SCHAUM
POP FAVORITES

ARRANGED BY WESLEY SCHAUM

CONTENTS

Art: Christine Pruett
Editor: Carole Flatau

Moondance

Words and Music by VAN MORRISON
Arranged by WESLEY SCHAUM

3

EL9528

Friends and Lovers
(Both to Each Other)

Words and Music by
PAUL GORDON and JAY GRUSKA
Arranged by WESLEY SCHAUM

Andante

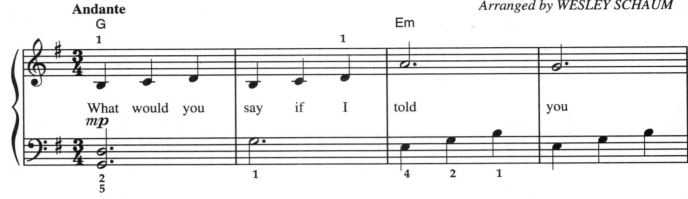

What would you say if I told you

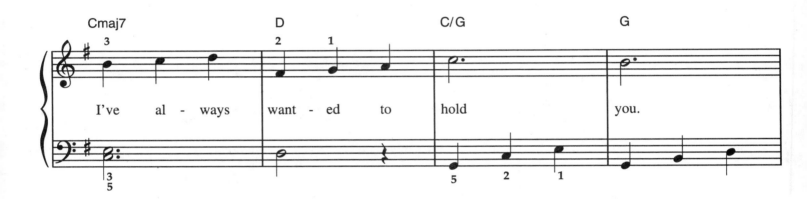

I've al - ways want - ed to hold you.

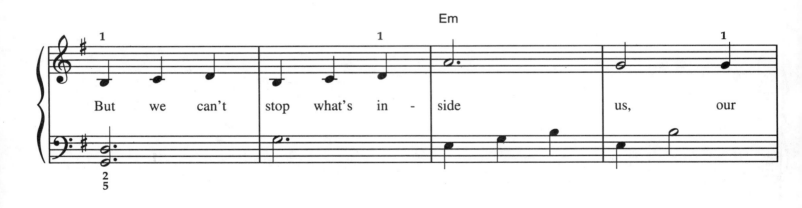

But we can't stop what's in - side us, our

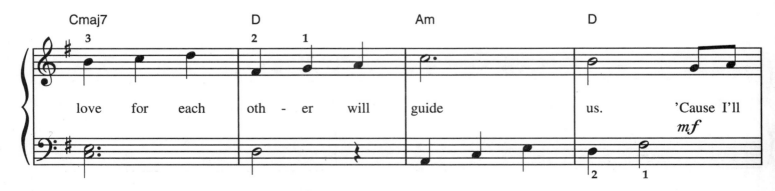

love for each oth - er will guide us. 'Cause I'll

Blues in the Night
(My Mama Done Tol' Me)

Words by JOHNNY MERCER

Music by HAROLD ARLEN
Arranged by WESLEY SCHAUM

My ma-ma done tol' me when I was in pig-tails,

My ma-ma done tol' me,

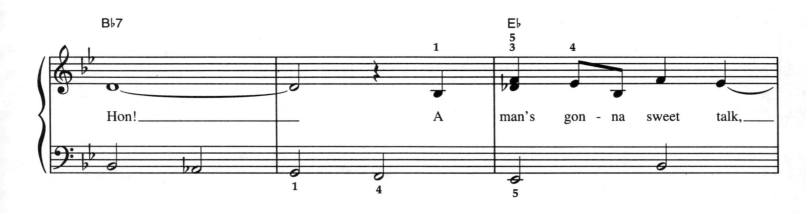

Hon! A man's gon-na sweet talk,

and give ya the big eye,

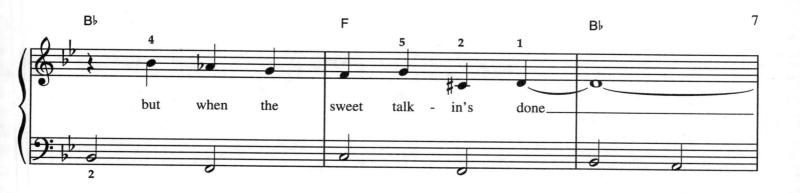

but when the sweet talk - in's done____

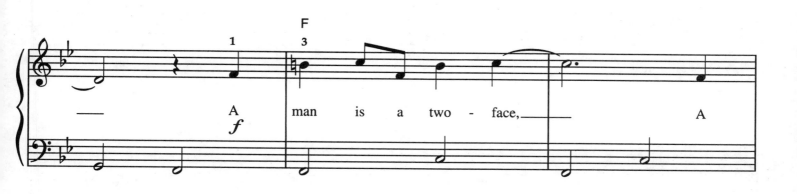

____ man is a two - face,____ A

wor - ri - some thing who'll leave ya t' sing the blues____

____ in the night.

Eye of the Tiger
(The Theme from "ROCKY III")

Words and Music by
FRANKIE SULLIVAN III
and JIM PETERIK
Arranged by WESLEY SCHAUM

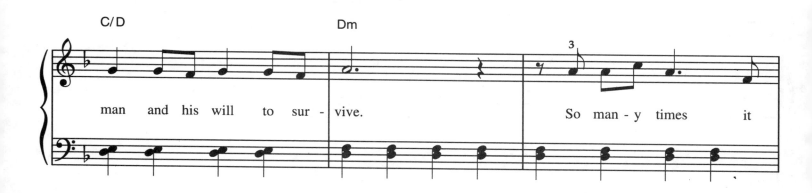

Don't Sit Under the Apple Tree
(With Anyone Else but Me)

Words and Music by
LEW BROWN, CHARLES TOBIAS
and SAM H. STEPT
Arranged by WESLEY SCHAUM

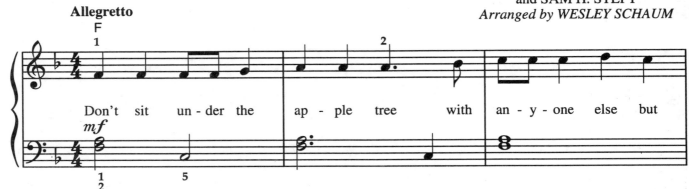

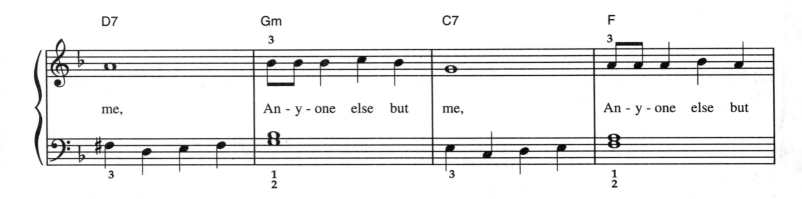

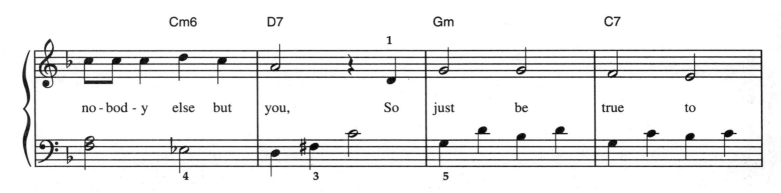

EL9528

11

Never My Love

Words and Music by
DON and DICK ADDRISI
Arranged by WESLEY SCHAUM

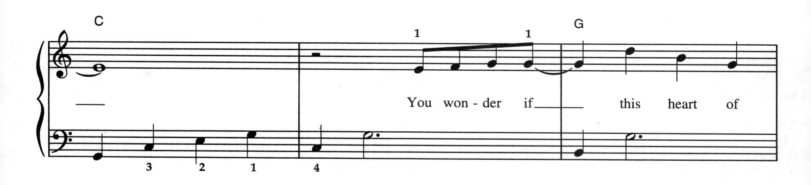

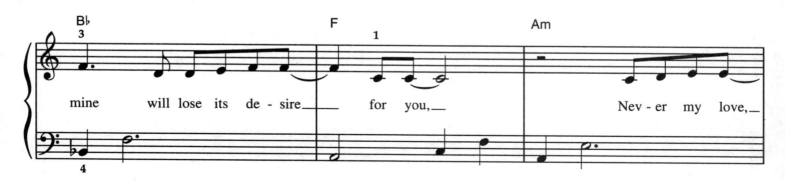

Rhinestone Cowboy

Words and Music by LARRY WEISS
Arranged by WESLEY SCHAUM

I'm gon - na be where the lights are shin - in' on me;

Like a rhine-stone cow - boy___ rid - ing out on a horse in a

star span-gled ro - de - o.___ Rhine-stone cow - boy,___

___ get - tin' cards and let - ters from peo - ple I don't e - ven

know; of - fers com-ing o - ver the phone.___

Jailhouse Rock

Words and Music by
JERRY LEIBER and MIKE STOLLER
Arranged by WESLEY SCHAUM

Can You Stop the Rain?

Words by JOHN BETTIS

Music by WALTER AFANASIEFF
Arranged by WESLEY SCHAUM

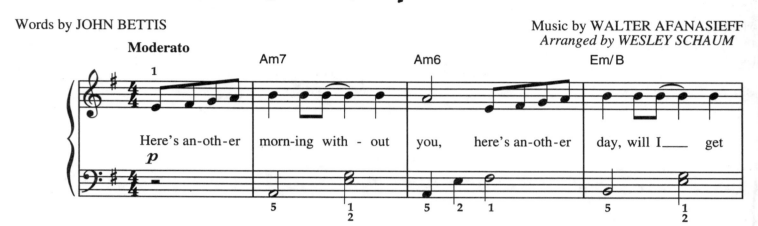

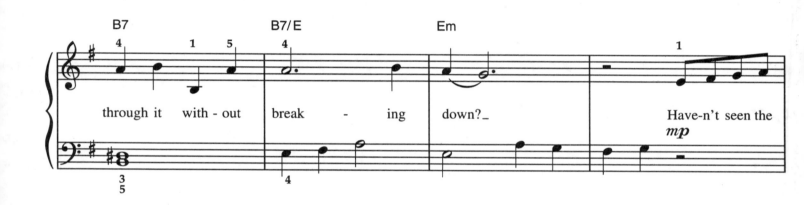

EL9528

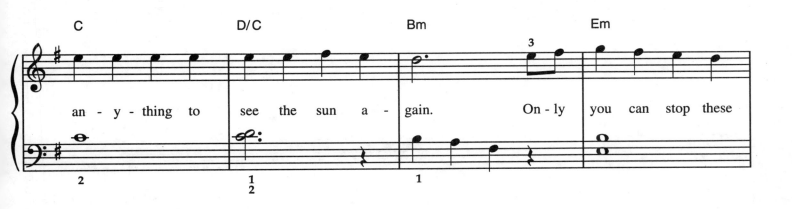

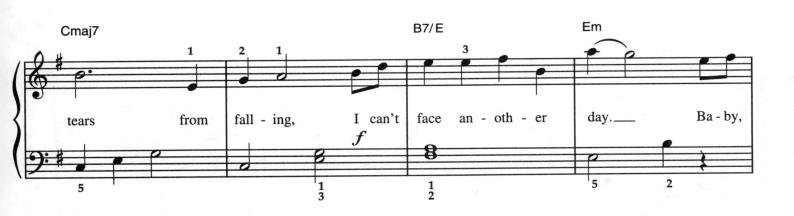

Alexander's Ragtime Band

Words and Music by IRVING BERLIN
Arranged by WESLEY SCHAUM

EL9528

Dream

Words and Music by
JOHNNY MERCER
Arranged by WESLEY SCHAUM

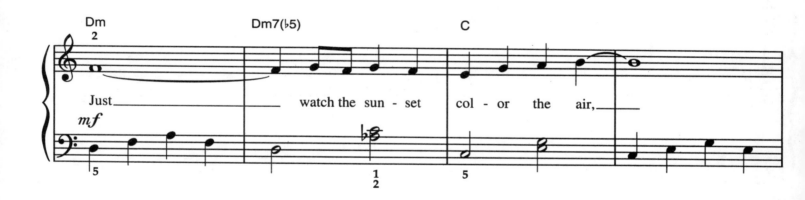

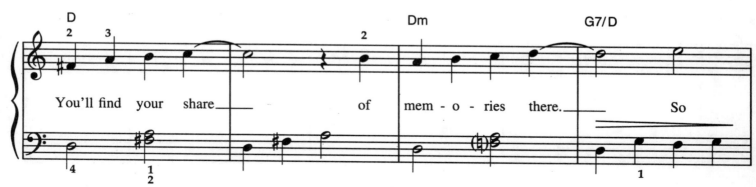

EL9528

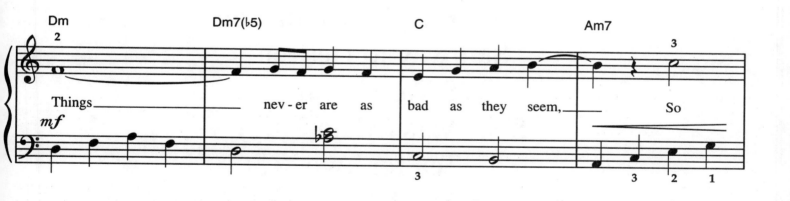

EL9528

SCHAUM
POP FAVORITES

ARRANGED BY WESLEY SCHAUM

EL9529

Begin the Beguine
Evergreen
I Only Have Eyes for You
Stairway to Heaven
'S Wonderful
Star Wars (Main Title)
Tea for Two
Theme from "A Summer Place"
The Thorn Birds (Main Theme)
The Wind Beneath My Wings
Your Smiling Face